THIS SELF-CARE

GUIDED JOURNAL

BELONGS TO:

Welcome to The Adult ADHD Self-Care Guided Journal.

There are very few habits which can positively impact as many different areas of your life as journaling. From calming anxiety to building self-esteem and from better sleep to increased productivity, the benefits are proven.

I've created this journal to give you a place to write, reflect, vent, and explore your thoughts and feelings. It's designed to work alongside 'The Adult ADHD Self-Care Handbook': all the prompts from the book are included here, as well as additional prompts and activities to support your self-care journey. If you prefer, you can also use it as a stand-alone journal.

There's no right or wrong way to use these pages — skip around, spend time on the parts that resonate with you, or simply do some coloring and let your mind wander. This is your space. Take your time with it, and make it your own. I'm so glad you're here, and I hope this journal helps you care for yourself in the ways you deserve.

Warmly,
Caroline

PS I have left a blank page after each coloring page: if you're using markers, it's also a good idea to place a sheet of paper behind the image you're coloring.

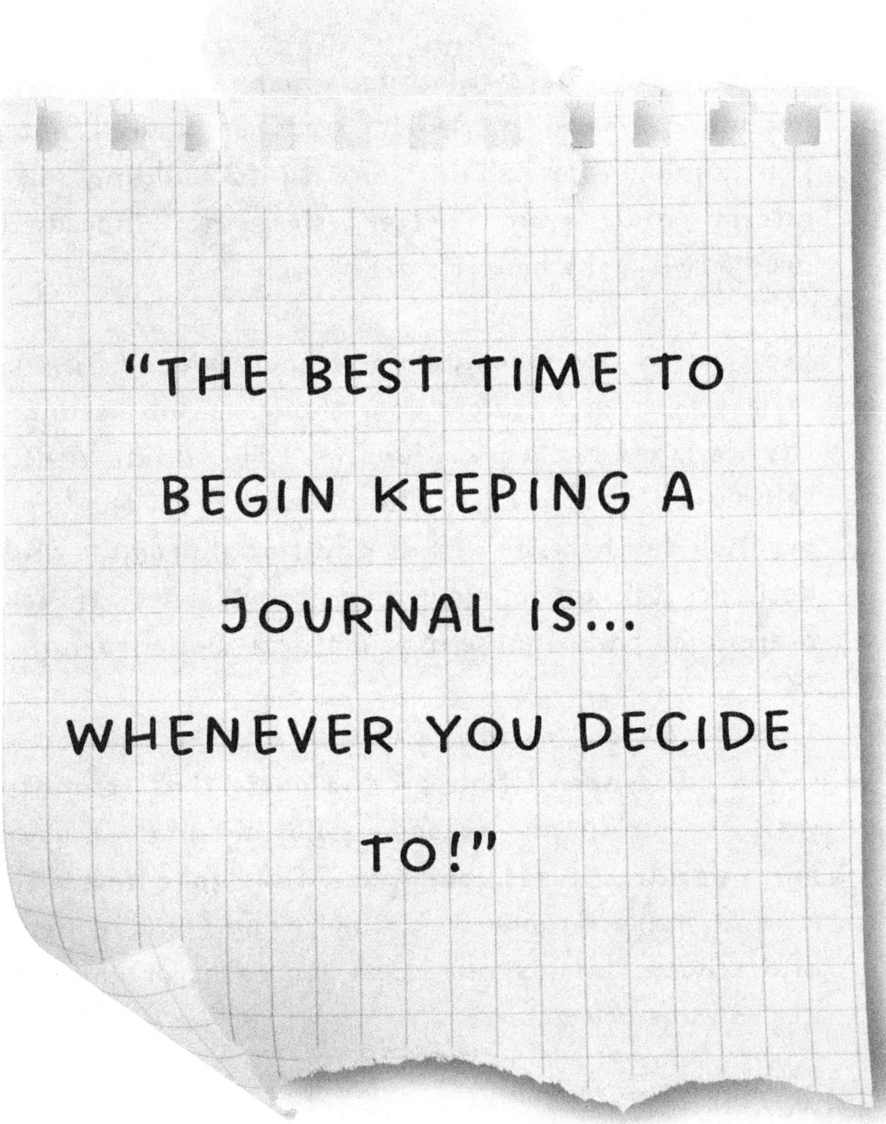
"THE BEST TIME TO
BEGIN KEEPING A
JOURNAL IS...
WHENEVER YOU DECIDE
TO!"

SECTION ONE: SOCIALIZING, RELATIONSHIPS AND COMMUNICATION

Welcome to the first section of this guided journal. If you're using it alongside 'The Adult ADHD Self-Care Handbook', this section pairs with Chapters 2-7 of the book.

In this section, you'll find prompts and reflections to guide you in exploring your social and relational experiences. You'll be encouraged to reflect on some of the challenges you might encounter in socializing, and why it can feel difficult at times.

There's space to explore habits like oversharing and avoiding phone calls, with ideas for how to navigate these challenges.

You'll also find prompts to help you think about ways to build and sustain meaningful friendships and nurture your relationship with your life partner.

THINK ABOUT A TIME WHEN YOU FELT CONFIDENT IN A SOCIAL SITUATION. WHAT MADE IT GO WELL? HOW DID YOU FEEL AFTERWARDS?

ON THE NEXT PAGE YOU WILL FIND SOME CONVERSATION STARTERS. WRITE DOWN THREE OF YOUR FAVORITE NEUTRAL, OPEN-ENDED QUESTIONS. YOU CAN USE THESE AT ANY TIME TO KEEP A CONVERSATION FLOWING.

Your Small Talk Cheat Sheet

Here are 10 neutral yet intriguing open-ended questions- great for getting a conversation started.

1. What's something you're really passionate about right now?
2. What's the most interesting thing you've learned recently?
3. What do you enjoy doing in your free time?
4. If you could travel anywhere in the world, where would you go and why?
5. If you were given a billion dollars right now, what would you do?
6. What's a hobby or activity you've always wanted to try?
7. Is there a book, movie, or show that has inspired you recently?
8. If you could have dinner with anyone, dead or alive, who would it be, and why?
9. Do you have a goal you're currently working toward?
10. What's the best advice you've ever received?

WHAT MAKES YOU FEEL ANXIOUS ABOUT TALKING TO NEW PEOPLE? WRITE DOWN THE SPECIFIC THOUGHTS OR FEARS THAT COME INTO YOUR MIND WHEN YOU ARE IN A SOCIAL SETTING. WHAT'S THE WORST THAT COULD HAPPEN? HOW MIGHT YOU REMIND YOURSELF THAT IT'S OKAY TO FEEL A LITTLE NERVOUS?

THINK ABOUT SOMEONE YOU ADMIRE FOR THEIR SOCIAL SKILLS. WHAT DO YOU NOTICE ABOUT THE WAY THEY INTERACT WITH OTHERS?

WHAT'S YOUR GO-TO STORY OR TOPIC WHEN YOU'RE NERVOUS IN SOCIAL SETTINGS?

SET A SMALL SOCIAL GOAL FOR YOURSELF THIS WEEK. WHETHER IT'S TALKING TO A STRANGER AT A COFFEE SHOP OR INITIATING A CONVERSATION WITH A COLLEAGUE, WRITE DOWN WHAT YOU HOPE TO GAIN FROM THE EXPERIENCE. HOW WILL YOU CELEBRATE TAKING THAT STEP?

HOW DO YOU REACT WHEN YOU'RE UNSURE HOW TO END A CONVERSATION?

REFLECT ON WHAT TYPICALLY HAPPENS WHEN YOU FEEL "STUCK" IN A SOCIAL SITUATION. WHAT PHRASES OR STRATEGIES COULD HELP YOU EXIT POLITELY WHILE KEEPING THINGS POSITIVE?

VISUALIZE YOUR MOST CONFIDENT SELF IN A SOCIAL SITUATION. HOW DO YOU STAND? WHAT DOES YOUR VOICE SOUND LIKE? IMAGINE YOURSELF HANDLING A CONVERSATION SMOOTHLY AND WRITE DOWN THE STEPS YOU COULD TAKE TO BECOME THAT VERSION OF YOURSELF.

I AM LOVED

Thinking about oversharing and how to avoid it...

REFLECT ON A RECENT CONVERSATION WHERE YOU FELT THAT YOU OVERSHARED. WHAT WAS THE SITUATION, AND WHAT TRIGGERED THE OVERSHARING? WHAT MIGHT YOU DO DIFFERENTLY NEXT TIME?

REFLECT ON YOUR BOUNDARIES: THINK ABOUT CONVERSATIONS YOU'VE HAD WHERE YOU LATER FELT VULNERABLE, EXPOSED, OR LIKE YOU SAID TOO MUCH. WHAT SPECIFIC TOPICS DID YOU SHARE THAT MADE YOU FEEL THIS WAY?

CREATE A LIST OF "OFF-LIMITS" TOPICS: WRITE DOWN 3-5 PERSONAL TOPICS OR STORIES THAT YOU'D PREFER TO KEEP PRIVATE. THESE ARE THINGS YOU'LL ONLY SHARE WITH CERTAIN PEOPLE OR SPECIFIC SITUATIONS.

STAY
POSITIVE

Thinking about friendships and how to keep them...

WHAT DO YOU VALUE MOST IN YOUR FRIENDSHIPS?

HOW DO YOU TYPICALLY FEEL ABOUT MAINTAINING FRIENDSHIPS? WHAT ARE THE CHALLENGES YOU HAVE IN KEEPING IN TOUCH WITH FRIENDS?

WHAT SPECIFIC FEELINGS COME UP WHEN YOU THINK ABOUT REACHING OUT OR MAKING PLANS?

ARE THERE SPECIFIC FRIENDSHIPS THAT YOU STRUGGLE TO MAINTAIN MORE THAN OTHERS? WHY?

WHAT PATTERNS DO YOU NOTICE IN YOUR SOCIAL BEHAVIOR? DO YOU TEND TO WITHDRAW DURING STRESSFUL TIMES? ARE YOU ABLE TO BE MORE SOCIAL WHEN YOU FEEL ENERGETIC?

WHAT TRIGGERS YOUR AVOIDANCE WHEN IT COMES TO SOCIALIZING OR COMMUNICATION?
IS IT ANXIETY, FEAR OF REJECTION, GUILT, OR SOMETHING ELSE?

WHEN WAS THE LAST TIME YOU AVOIDED CONNECTING WITH A FRIEND?
WHO WAS IT, AND WHAT WAS THE REASON?

I AM
A FRIEND

WHAT EMOTIONS DO YOU FEEL WHEN YOU HAVE TO MAKE OR RECEIVE A PHONE CALL? IS IT ANXIETY, OVERWHELM, OR DREAD? WHAT ARE THE SPECIFIC THOUGHTS AND FEELINGS THAT ARISE, AND WHY?

WHAT ARE SOME ALTERNATIVES TO PHONE CALLS THAT YOU FEEL MORE COMFORTABLE WITH? WHAT COULD MAKE PHONE CALLS EASIER OR LESS STRESSFUL FOR YOU?

WHAT SMALL STEPS CAN YOU TAKE TO STAY CONNECTED WITH FRIENDS IN A WAY THAT FEELS MORE MANAGEABLE THAN MAKING OR RESPONDING TO A PHONE CALL?

RECORD YOUR WINS HERE:

POSITIVE AND SPECIAL

WHAT ARE YOUR BIGGEST COMMUNICATION CHALLENGES WHEN INTERACTING WITH LOVED ONES? HOW DO YOU THINK ADHD AFFECTS THESE CHALLENGES?

REFLECT ON A RECENT CONVERSATION WITH YOUR PARTNER THAT WENT WELL. WHAT MADE IT SUCCESSFUL? HOW DID YOU STAY FOCUSED AND ENGAGED?

ARE THERE SPECIFIC SITUATIONS OR TOPICS THAT TRIGGER CONFLICTS OR MISUNDERSTANDINGS?

WHEN YOU'RE FEELING OVERWHELMED OR DISTRACTED, HOW DO YOU COMMUNICATE YOUR NEEDS TO YOUR PARTNER OR LOVED ONES? HOW CAN YOU IMPROVE THIS?

DESCRIBE A SITUATION WHERE YOU FELT MISUNDERSTOOD BY YOUR PARTNER BECAUSE OF HOW ADHD AFFECTS YOUR COMMUNICATION. HOW DID YOU RESPOND, AND WHAT MIGHT HELP IN THE FUTURE?

WHAT DOES ACTIVE LISTENING MEAN TO YOU? WHAT STRATEGIES CAN YOU IMPLEMENT TO IMPROVE YOUR ACTIVE LISTENING SKILLS?

IF YOU COULD ASK YOUR PARTNER OR LOVED ONE FOR ONE SPECIFIC TYPE OF SUPPORT, WHAT WOULD IT BE AND WHY?

YOU'RE
BRAVER
THAN YOU
BELIEVE,
STRONGER
THAN YOU
SEEM AND
SMARTER
THAN YOU
THINK

SECTION TWO: MINDFULNESS AND EMOTIONAL DECLUTTERING

Welcome to Section Two of this journal. If you're using it alongside 'The Adult ADHD Self-Care Handbook', this section complements Chapters 8-10.

In this part of the journal, you'll discover calming breathing exercises and mindfulness practices to explore at your own pace. You'll reflect on what techniques resonate most with you, and consider simple ways to bring mindfulness into your daily life.

This section also provides prompts to help you process and release any emotions you might be carrying. Think of this journal as a safe haven, where you can express yourself freely and transform those feelings into clarity and calm.

WHEN YOU ARE FEELING STRESSED OR OVERWHELMED, TRY ONE OF THE VERY SIMPLE BREATHING EXERCISES OVERLEAF. DESCRIBE HOW IT FELT AND ANY CHANGES YOU NOTICED IN YOUR BODY OR MIND. HOW DID THIS SHORT EXERCISE IMPACT YOUR FOCUS OR MOOD?

THINK OF AN EVERYDAY ACTIVITY E.G., WALKING, BRUSHING YOUR TEETH, OR PREPARING A MEAL. HOW MIGHT YOU APPLY MINDFULNESS TO THIS TASK?

Three Simple and Easy Breathing Exercises.

Deep belly breathing activates the parasympathetic nervous system, which helps calm the body and mind.

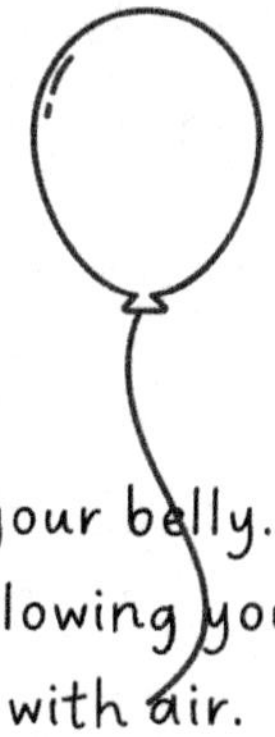

Balloon belly breathing

1. Sit or lie down in a comfortable position.
2. Place one hand on your chest and the other on your belly.
3. Take a slow, deep breath in through your nose, allowing your belly to swell like a balloon as you fill your lungs with air.
4. Hold your breath for a moment, then exhale slowly through your mouth, like you are blowing up a balloon.
5. Repeat this process several times, focusing on the rise and fall of your belly.

Box breathing

1. Sit or lie comfortably. Inhale for four seconds, hold the breath for four seconds, exhale for four seconds.
2. Repeat, inhale, hold the breath and exhale again for four seconds each time. It's simple but powerful, helping to regulate your breathing and bring a sense of calm.

4-7-8 breathing

Inhale for four seconds, hold the breath for seven seconds, and then exhale for eight seconds. This extended exhale helps to release tension, reduce anxiety and promote relaxation.

Mindful eating

Mindful eating is a simple practice that can transform your relationship with food and improve your focus and enjoyment during meals.

1. Take a small snack, like a piece of fruit or a handful of nuts.
2. Focus on looking at the food: notice its texture, smell, color.
3. Eat slowly, experiencing the taste and texture as you chew. Set aside distractions like phones or TV. Try to recognize when you're satisfied.

Body scan meditation

1. When you have 10 minutes to spare, without interruptions or distractions, start by finding a comfortable position, either sitting or lying down.
2. Close your eyes and take a few deep breaths to settle into the moment.
3. Begin by focusing on the top of your head, noticing any sensations or tension.
4. Gradually move your attention down to your face, neck, shoulders, and so on, until you reach your toes.
5. Spend a few moments on each body part, simply observing any physical sensations, like warmth, tingling, or tightness.

Practicing body scan meditation for 5 or 10 minutes daily can increase body awareness and relaxation, helping you stay grounded and centered.

I AM BLESSED

A JOURNAL LIKE THIS IS IDEAL FOR HEALTHY VENTING. THIS IS YOUR SPACE TO LET GO OF EMOTIONS AND FEELINGS YOU HAVE BEEN BOTTLING UP FOR TOO LONG, AND THAT ARE CAUSING YOU STRESS AND ANXIETY.

START WITH ONE OF THESE SIMPLE PROMPTS:
"I'M FEELING OVERWHELMED RIGHT NOW BECAUSE..."

I NEED TO GET THIS OUT: WHAT'S REALLY BOTHERING ME IS...

IF I COULD YELL AT SOMETHING OR SOMEONE (WITHOUT CONSEQUENCES), I'D SAY...

TODAY, I'M SO MAD BECAUSE...

I'VE BEEN HOLDING THIS IN FOR TOO LONG: IT'S TIME TO SAY...

I NEED TO VENT ABOUT THIS SITUATION: HERE'S WHAT'S BEEN HAPPENING...

I CAN DO THIS

IF MY FEELINGS COULD SPEAK, THEY WOULD SAY...

IT CAN BE VERY HELPFUL TO WRITE YOURSELF A VENTING LETTER, RELEASING ALL YOUR FRUSTRATIONS AND WORRIES ONTO THE PAGE.

SOME PROMPTS FOR WRITING
A VENTING LETTER:

- WHAT'S BEEN WEIGHING ON YOUR MIND THE MOST LATELY?
- WHAT DO YOU WISH SOMEONE ELSE COULD UNDERSTAND ABOUT HOW YOU'RE FEELING?
- IF YOU COULD TELL THE PERSON WHO'S BEEN STRESSING YOU OUT EXACTLY WHAT YOU FEEL, WHAT WOULD YOU SAY?
- HOW HAVE YOU BEEN PUSHING YOURSELF TOO HARD?
- WHAT'S ONE THING YOU WANT TO REMIND YOURSELF ABOUT THIS SITUATION?

NOW, TAKE A DEEP BREATH AND START WRITING...

Never
STOP
Growing

SECTION THREE: BUILDING SELF- ESTEEM AND BANISHING NEGATIVE SELF-TALK.

Welcome to Section Three of this journal. If you're currently exploring the 'Adult ADHD Self-Care Handbook,' this section aligns with Chapters 11-13.

The focus here will be on cultivating self-esteem and dismantling negative self-talk, alongside tackling Rejection Sensitive Dysphoria (RSD) and perfectionism, which are common challenges for many with ADHD.

Within these pages, you'll engage with prompts designed to transform your negative thought patterns and foster self-compassion. Use this journal as a safe space to start confronting deep-seated emotions and thoughts. Once you understand them better, you can start to reduce their impact on your well-being.

Thinking about self-esteem and how to cultivate it...

NAME THREE STRENGTHS OR POSITIVE QUALITIES YOU POSSESS THAT MIGHT BE LINKED TO ADHD. HOW DO THESE STRENGTHS HELP YOU IN DAILY LIFE?

LIST FIVE THINGS YOU LIKE ABOUT YOURSELF THAT HAVE NOTHING TO DO WITH YOUR PRODUCTIVITY OR HOW WELL YOU MANAGE YOUR ADHD.

WHAT NEGATIVE THOUGHTS DO YOU OFTEN HAVE ABOUT YOURSELF BECAUSE OF YOUR ADHD? HOW TRUE ARE THESE THOUGHTS, REALLY?

CHOOSE ONE RECURRING NEGATIVE THOUGHT ABOUT YOURSELF AND REFRAME IT IN A MORE POSITIVE OR COMPASSIONATE WAY. HOW MIGHT THIS NEW PERSPECTIVE CHANGE THE WAY YOU FEEL ABOUT YOURSELF?

DO YOU TEND TO COMPARE YOURSELF TO OTHERS? ANYONE IN PARTICULAR, AND WHY?

HOW DOES THIS COMPARISON IMPACT YOUR SELF-WORTH?

YOU ARE
amazing

WRITE DOWN YOUR 5 FAVORITE POSITIVE AFFIRMATIONS FROM THE LIST ON THE NEXT PAGE. ONCE YOU HAVE YOUR LIST, MAKE IT A HABIT TO REPEAT THESE AFFIRMATIONS REGULARLY. TAKE A FEW MINUTES EACH DAY TO RE-READ THEM AND REFLECT ON WHAT THEY MEAN TO YOU.

15 Affirmations for Self-Compassion

Here are 15 Positive Affirmations that work to he boost self-esteem and self acceptance.

- I am on my own unique journey, and I trust the timing of my life.
- Another person's success does not take away from my own potential.
- I am proud of my progress, no matter how small it may seem.
- I am capable of achieving great things in my ow way and time.

- I am enough as I am, and m worth is not defined by extern achievements.
- I have valuable strengths and ski that are uniquely mine.

- I am deserving of love, success, and happiness, just as much as anyone else.
- I acknowledge my efforts and growth, and I choose to focus on my own path.
- I am resilient, and I have the power to improve my situation one step at a time.
- Even when things feel hard, I believe in my ability to keep going.
- I can create the life I want, and I trust that I will find my way.
- Challenges are opportunities for growth, and I am capable of learning from them.
- I focus on my own progress, knowing that small steps lead to big change.
- I am improving and growing each day, even if I can't always see it.
- I am capable of achieving what matters to me, one step at a time.

WHAT SPECIFIC SITUATIONS TEND TO TRIGGER FEELINGS OF REJECTION OR SENSITIVITY FOR YOU?

IS IT MORE RELATED TO CRITICISM, SOCIAL REJECTION, OR FEAR OF FAILURE?

THINK ABOUT A RECENT SITUATION WHERE YOU FELT REJECTED. WAS IT BASED ON SOMETHING SOMEONE EXPLICITLY SAID OR DID, OR WAS IT MORE ABOUT YOUR INTERPRETATION OF THE EVENT?

HOW MIGHT YOUR OWN PERCEPTION OF YOURSELF INFLUENCE THE WAY YOU FEEL ABOUT FEEDBACK OR CRITICISM?

WHAT ARE SOME AUTOMATIC THOUGHTS YOU HAVE WHEN YOU FEEL REJECTED? HOW CAN YOU CHANNEL THESE THOUGHTS INTO SOMETHING MORE COMPASSIONATE AND REALISTIC?

WHAT COPING MECHANISMS OR STRATEGIES HAVE HELPED YOU MANAGE FEELINGS OF REJECTION OR SENSITIVITY IN THE PAST? HOW CAN YOU USE THEM MORE CONSISTENTLY WHEN RSD ARISES?

ARE THERE SITUATIONS OR OPPORTUNITIES YOU AVOID BECAUSE YOU FEAR REJECTION OR CRITICISM? WHAT MIGHT HAPPEN IF YOU TOOK A SMALL RISK AND FACED ONE OF THESE SITUATIONS HEAD-ON?

CREATE YOUR SELF-COMPASSION TOOLKIT: LIST 5 OR 6 ACTIVITIES YOU CAN GO TO FOR REASSURANCE AND AN UPLIFT WHEN YOU ARE TEMPTED TO SINK INTO NEGATIVITY. WE CALL THESE 'GLIMMERS': ACTIVITIES, PEOPLE, HOBBIES OR SIMPLE PLEASURES THAT SPARK JOY, CHEER YOU UP AND GIVE COMFORT WHEN THE WORLD FEELS TOO DIFFICULT.

HAVE A LOOK AT THE IDEAS ON THE NEXT PAGE, AND WRITE DOWN YOUR OWN FAVORITES.

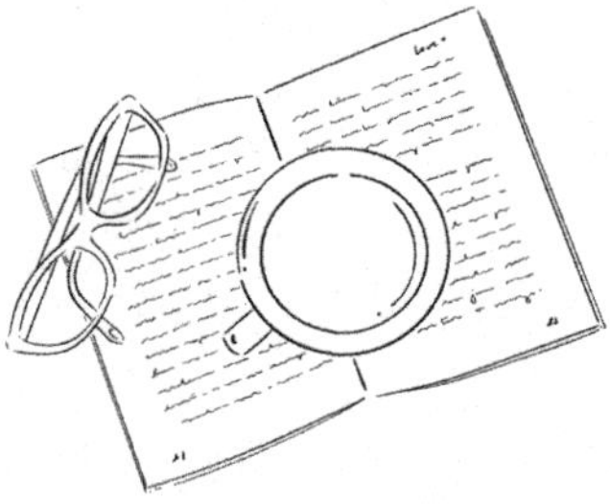

Identify your Glimmers

A glimmer is the opposite of a trigger. A trigger is something that causes stress and anxiety, while a glimmer is something small and simple that you can do that has a calming, stabilizing effect and creates a positive reaction. Here are some ideas:

- Take a stroll in Nature - fresh air can help you clear your mind and improve your mood.
- Guided daydreaming, where you picture yourself in a tranquil place; maybe a quiet beach or a lush forest.
- Aromatherapy: Light some scented candles or use essential oils with calming scents like lavender or chamomile.
- Coloring is relaxing and can really help you zone out when you are feeling anxious. Crafts like knitting, crocheting, and scrapbooking are fun, and you get to create something beautiful as an outlet for your feelings.
- Put on some soft music or your favorite audiobook or podcast to help take your mind off the stress.
- Do some gentle yoga or simple stretching. It's not only good for your body but also helps quieten your mind.

HOW DO YOU TYPICALLY TREAT YOURSELF AFTER EXPERIENCING REJECTION OR CRITICISM? ARE YOU KIND AND UNDERSTANDING, OR DO YOU TEND TO BE HARSH AND CRITICAL WITH YOURSELF?
WHAT WOULD IT LOOK LIKE TO PRACTICE SELF-COMPASSION IN THOSE MOMENTS?

WRITE A LETTER TO YOURSELF FROM THE PERSPECTIVE OF A KIND AND SUPPORTIVE FRIEND AFTER YOU'VE EXPERIENCED REJECTION. WHAT ENCOURAGING WORDS OR ADVICE WOULD THIS FRIEND OFFER TO HELP YOU FEEL BETTER?

WHAT BOUNDARIES CAN YOU SET WITH INDIVIDUALS OR SITUATIONS THAT TRIGGER FEELINGS OF REJECTION?

IF YOU COULD GO BACK AND OFFER ADVICE TO YOURSELF AFTER A PAINFUL REJECTION, WHAT WOULD YOU SAY?

HOW CAN YOU HELP YOUR FUTURE SELF TO MOVE FORWARD WITH MORE CONFIDENCE?

WHO ARE THE PEOPLE IN YOUR LIFE WHO MAKE YOU FEEL SAFE, SUPPORTED, AND VALUED, REGARDLESS OF YOUR PERCEIVED FLAWS OR FAILURES? HOW CAN YOU LEAN ON THEM FOR SUPPORT WHEN RSD FLARES UP?

YES
YOU
CAN

WHAT DOES "PERFECT" MEAN TO YOU? HOW HAS PERFECTIONISM IMPACTED YOUR GOALS OR ACTIONS?

WRITE ABOUT A TIME WHEN SOMETHING DIDN'T GO AS PLANNED, BUT THE OUTCOME WAS STILL POSITIVE OR VALUABLE.

WHAT ARE THREE THINGS YOUR INNER CRITIC SAYS WHEN YOU DON'T MEET YOUR STANDARDS? HOW CAN YOU REFRAME THEM?

MAKE A LIST OF 5 ACTIVITIES OR TASKS WHERE YOU CAN PRACTICE ACCEPTING "GOOD ENOUGH" INSTEAD OF STRIVING FOR PERFECT.

SET REALISTIC GOALS: CHOOSE ONE TASK OR PROJECT AND THINK ABOUT HOW YOU CAN BREAK IT INTO MANAGEABLE STEPS.

LIST FIVE ACCOMPLISHMENTS FROM THE PAST WEEK, NO MATTER HOW SMALL, AND DESCRIBE IN A FEW WORDS HOW THEY MADE YOU FEEL.

SECTION FOUR: UNMASKING, EMBRACING AUTHENTICITY AND SETTING BOUNDARIES

Welcome to Section Four of this journal. If you're reading 'The Adult ADHD Self-Care Handbook', this section complements Chapters 14 & 15.

Here, we'll focus on unmasking, embracing authenticity, and creating healthy boundaries. For many people with ADHD, masking – hiding parts of our true selves to fit in or avoid judgment – has been a long-standing habit. While it can sometimes be a survival tool, masking often comes at the cost of our mental and emotional well-being.

In this section, you'll find prompts to help you define your core values, explore the reasons behind your masking behaviors, and start to consider how and when you might begin unmasking safely. Additionally, you'll reflect on the role boundaries play in maintaining authenticity and protecting your energy.

WHAT DOES "AUTHENTICITY" MEAN TO YOU? WHAT ARE THE CORE VALUES THAT DEFINE YOUR TRUE SELF?
TAKE A LOOK AT THE CORE VALUES ON THE NEXT TWO PAGES. THINK ABOUT MOMENTS IN YOUR LIFE WHEN YOU FELT TRULY FULFILLED OR PROUD. WHAT WAS HAPPENING AT THOSE TIMES? THESE MOMENTS OFTEN ALIGN WITH CORE VALUES.

NOW, WRITE DOWN A LIST OF THE VALUES THAT MOST STRONGLY RESONATE WITH YOU. THERE'S NO RIGHT OR WRONG ANSWER, BUT TRY TO NARROW YOUR LIST DOWN TO 5-7 CORE VALUES THAT YOU BELIEVE SHOULD GUIDE YOU THE MOST.

Core Values

Here are some of the most important core values. Which ones resonate most with you?

- ·Authenticity - Being true to yourself and acting in ways that are consistent with your inner beliefs.
- Compassion - Showing kindness and empathy towards others, and being motivated to help those in need.
- Integrity - Acting honestly and ethically, even when it's difficult.
- Creativity - Valuing imagination, innovation, and expressing yourself in unique ways.
- Independence - Seeking freedom and autonomy in your decisions and lifestyle.
- Family - Prioritizing close relationships with family members and creating a supportive family environment.
- Growth - Always looking for opportunities to improve yourself, learn, and evolve.

- Connection - Building and maintaining meaningful relationships with others.
- Loyalty - Staying committed to the people and causes you care about.
- Courage - Facing fears and taking risks, especially when standing up for what you believe in.
- Adventure - Valuing new experiences, excitement, and exploration.
- Fairness - Seeking justice and equality in the way people are treated.
- Mindfulness - Being present and fully engaged in the moment, appreciating life's details.
- Curiosity - A desire to learn, explore new ideas, and understand the world better.
- Responsibility - Being accountable for your actions and their consequences.
- Peace - Valuing calmness, serenity, and a harmonious way of life.
- Humor - Valuing fun, laughter, and finding joy in life.

WHEN DO YOU FEEL MOST LIKE YOUR AUTHENTIC SELF?

REFLECT ON SPECIFIC MOMENTS WHEN YOU FEEL FREE TO BE YOURSELF. WHAT ACTIVITIES, PEOPLE, OR ENVIRONMENTS BRING OUT THE REAL YOU?

WHAT PARTS OF YOURSELF DO YOU TEND TO HIDE FROM OTHERS? WHY?

WRITE DOWN FIVE ASPECTS OF YOUR PERSONALITY OR ADHD TRAITS THAT YOU FEEL THE NEED TO MASK. WHAT FEARS OR BELIEFS LEAD TO THIS BEHAVIOR?

HOW DOES MASKING AFFECT YOUR EMOTIONAL WELL-BEING?

WRITE ABOUT HOW YOU FEEL AFTER MASKING YOUR ADHD TRAITS. DOES IT LEAVE YOU FEELING DRAINED, ANXIOUS, OR DISCONNECTED FROM YOURSELF?

WHO ARE THE PEOPLE IN YOUR LIFE WHO MAKE YOU FEEL SAFE AND UNDERSTOOD?

REFLECT ON THOSE WHO ENCOURAGE YOU TO BE YOUR AUTHENTIC SELF. HOW CAN YOU SPEND MORE TIME WITH THESE PEOPLE OR STRENGTHEN THOSE RELATIONSHIPS?

WHAT WOULD YOUR LIFE LOOK LIKE IF YOU EMBRACED YOUR AUTHENTIC SELF MORE OFTEN?

IMAGINE A FUTURE WHERE YOU ALLOW YOURSELF TO BE FULLY SEEN WITHOUT MASKING. HOW MIGHT THIS CHANGE YOUR RELATIONSHIPS, CAREER, OR DAILY LIFE?

THINK OF ONE THING YOU COULD DO TO START UNMASKING AND SHOWING YOUR TRUE SELF IN DAILY LIFE.

FOR EXAMPLE:

- BEING MORE HONEST ABOUT YOUR NEEDS
- SETTING BOUNDARIES
- CONTROLLING YOUR PEOPLE-PLEASING TENDENCIES
- EXPLAINING SOME OF YOUR ADHD TRAITS TO OTHERS.

HOW CAN YOU START TO DO THIS? WHERE WILL YOU BEGIN? WRITE DOWN A PLAN OF ACTION HERE:

WHAT SELF-COMPASSION PRACTICES CAN YOU USE TO SUPPORT YOURSELF DURING THE UNMASKING PROCESS?

THINK OF THE WAYS YOU CAN BE KINDER TO YOURSELF AS YOU REVEAL YOUR TRUE SELF.

Be your
own kind of
beautiful

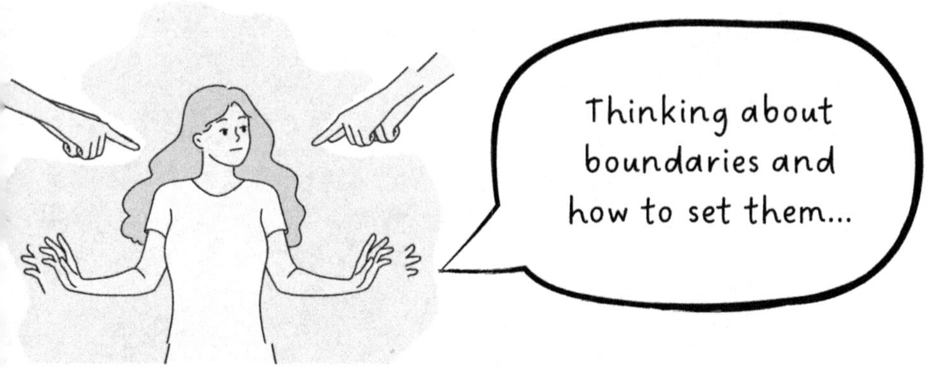

THINK OF A RECENT SITUATION WHERE YOU FELT OVERWHELMED, DISRESPECTED, OR EXHAUSTED.

WHAT WAS THE CONTEXT, AND WHO WAS INVOLVED?

WHAT ACTIVITIES OR COMMITMENTS CONSISTENTLY DRAIN YOUR ENERGY AND LEAVE YOU FEELING DEPLETED?

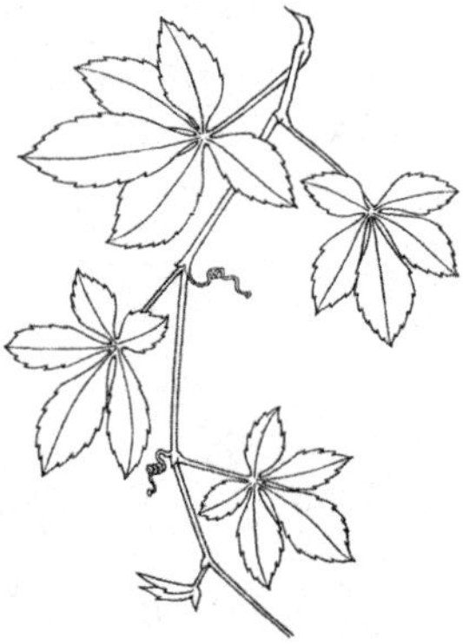

THINK ABOUT AREAS WHERE YOU'RE MOST PRONE TO SAY "YES" WHEN YOU WOULD PREFER TO SAY "NO." WHAT ARE THEY AND HOW CAN YOU CHANGE THIS PATTERN?

no rain
no flowers

TAKE A LOOK AT THE IDEAS ON THE FOLLOWING PAGE. CREATE A LIST OF NON-NEGOTIABLE BOUNDARIES FOR DIFFERENT AREAS OF YOUR LIFE.

USE CLEAR AND ACTIONABLE STATEMENTS STARTING WITH "I WILL" OR "I WILL NOT."

ENSURE THEY ARE REALISTIC AND ENFORCEABLE.

IF YOU THINK IT'S APPROPRIATE, SHARE THESE BOUNDARIES WITH THE PEOPLE CLOSE TO YOU.

Some Ideas for Boundaries that Work for You.

At work:

- Make it a rule that you will not check work emails after 6pm.
- Take a 30-minute lunch break every day without interruptions.

At home:

- Pledge to take some time each week to dedicate to self-care.
- Build in some alone time to re-charge each day.
- Offer to help others only when you feel emotionally and physically capable.

Social Life:

- Don't agree to more than, say, two social events per week.
- Make it a rule to slip away from social gatherings when you are feeling tired or overstimulated.
- Say no to events or commitments you don't have the mental or physical energy to attend.

Self-Care:

- Make it a priority to get 7 hours of sleep every night.
- Try to get 20 minutes of exercise three times a week
- Take time to journal regularly and be very conscious of not bottling up emotions.
- Pledge to communicate your needs to those around you, even if it means a difficult conversation.

Digital Life:

- No more than one hour scrolling social media daily.
- Consciously avoid oversharing personal details on social media, and avoid online arguments and negativity.

SECTION FIVE: EXPRESSING GRATITUDE AND THE ART OF THE BRAIN DUMP

Gratitude journaling is a simple yet powerful way to train our brains to focus on the positive. By intentionally shifting our attention to what we are thankful for, instead of what's bothering us, we can eliminate negativity and improve our mood.

Start small: make a conscious effort to write down three things you're grateful for every day, no matter how tiny they seem. Anything that brings a smile to your day.

To get you started, here are some gratitude prompts that will help to focus your mind on the positive. Simply pick one prompt each day and write down three answers. It can be the same prompt each time, or a different one every day - whatever speaks to you most strongly at the time.

GRATITUDE PROMPTS

- TODAY I NOTICED THIS AND IT MADE ME SMILE
- TODAY I LAUGHED BECAUSE...
- TODAY I SAW A BEAUTIFUL...
- TODAY I HAD THE COURAGE TO...
- TODAY I LEARNED...
- I KNOW I AM STRONG BECAUSE...
- 3 PEOPLE I AM GRATEFUL FOR ARE...
- 3 EXPERIENCES I AM GRATEFUL FOR ARE...
- 3 SKILLS I AM GRATEFUL FOR ARE...
- TODAY I FELT HAPPY WHEN...
- TODAY I FELT CONNECTED TO OTHERS WHEN...
- TODAY I FELT UNDERSTOOD WHEN...
- I KNOW I AM SUPPORTED BECAUSE...
- I KNOW I AM GROWING BECAUSE...
- I KNOW I AM STRONG BECAUSE...

gratitude CHANGES everything

Choose
TO BE
GRATEFUL

THE BRAIN DUMP

A brain dump is the process of transferring all the thoughts, ideas, tasks, and worries swirling around in our minds onto paper. It helps to clear mental clutter, reduce overwhelm, and make room for focused thinking.

Begin by jotting down everything on your mind - tasks, ideas, worries, or reminders, without worrying about how it's structured or whether it makes sense. Let your thoughts flow freely and focus on simply getting everything out of your head.

Once you've written everything down, take a short break to clear your mind. Then review your list and try to organize it by grouping similar items together, highlighting priorities, or sorting tasks into categories like "urgent" or "later".

Finally, use your brain dump as a reference so you can turn it into the basis of an actionable plan.

ALL THE STUFF I NEED TO DUMP OUT OF MY BRAIN RIGHT NOW:

ACTION STEPS:

ALL THE STUFF I NEED TO DUMP OUT OF MY BRAIN RIGHT NOW:

ACTION STEPS:

ALL THE STUFF I NEED TO DUMP OUT OF MY BRAIN RIGHT NOW:

ACTION STEPS:

YOUR SLEEP TRACKER

If you have trouble sleeping, it's a good idea to track your sleep for a week or two, so that you can start to identify patterns or factors that might affect your sleep, such as stress, diet or pre-bedtime habits.

Using the prompts on the following page, grab a notebook and record the time you go to bed, the time you wake up, and any awakenings during the night. Note down how you feel in the morning and any factors that might have affected your sleep.

Over time, you'll notice patterns that can help you identify what works best for you. For example, you might find that you sleep better on days when you exercise, or that certain foods or activities disrupt your sleep.

DAILY SLEEP LOG PROMPTS

WHAT TIME DID YOU GO TO BED LAST NIGHT?

WHAT TIME DID YOU FALL ASLEEP? (ESTIMATE IF UNSURE)

WHAT TIME DID YOU WAKE UP?

TOTAL HOURS OF SLEEP:

HOW RESTED DO YOU FEEL THIS MORNING? (1-10 SCALE OR A SHORT NOTE)

DID YOU WAKE UP DURING THE NIGHT? IF SO, HOW MANY TIMES AND FOR HOW LONG?

WHAT WAS YOUR LAST THOUGHT BEFORE FALLING ASLEEP?

DID YOU HAVE ANY DREAMS? JOT DOWN ANY YOU REMEMBER.

WHAT'S YOUR MORNING MOOD?

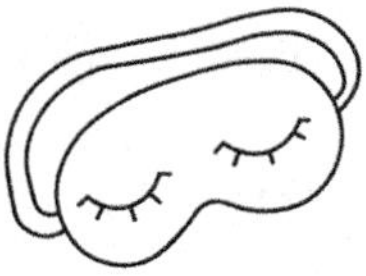

WHAT DID YOU DO IN THE HOUR BEFORE BED?

DID YOU CONSUME CAFFEINE, SUGAR, OR ALCOHOL IN THE EVENING?

DID YOU TAKE ANY SUPPLEMENTS OR MEDICATION?

WAS YOUR SLEEP ENVIRONMENT COMFORTABLE?

DID YOU USE ANY SLEEP AIDS? (WHITE NOISE, WEIGHTED BLANKET, ETC.)

WHAT SLEEP HABITS HELP YOU THE MOST?

WHAT DISRUPTS YOUR SLEEP THE MOST?

IF YOU HAD A BAD SLEEP, WHAT MIGHT HAVE CONTRIBUTED TO IT?

IF YOU HAD A GOOD SLEEP, WHAT DO YOU THINK HELPED?

WHAT'S ONE SMALL CHANGE YOU CAN TRY TO IMPROVE YOUR SLEEP THIS WEEK?

Anything
is
Possible

Discover Your Next Coloring Escape!

If coloring is one of your go-to ways to de-stress and take time out from the hustle and bustle of the day, get ready to fall in love with the *Super-Easy Stress Relief Coloring Book*.

Inside, you'll find beautifully crafted, simple-to-color mandalas, inspiring quotes and affirmations, adorable birds and butterflies, and delightful floral designs. Each page is designed to help you relax and unwind.

Get your copy by scanning the code here.

Scan me!

Printed in Dunstable, United Kingdom

76329589R00067